Supervising Youth Workers

The Potential and Pitfalls for Churches Employing Youth Workers

Malcolm Herbert
Director of Ordinands and Curate Training,
Diocese of Bristol

Sally Nash
Director of the Midlands Centre for Youth Ministry

GROVE BOOKS LIMITED
RIDLEY HALL RD CAMBRIDGE CB3 9HU

Contents

Malcolm's Acknowledgments

Thanks to all who inspired and encouraged me in this project, especially to Dr Pete Ward and other youth ministry practitioners who have opened my eyes to seeing ministry from a fresh perspective. Special thanks to Sally for the wealth of experience and wisdom she has brought to this project and to Sheryl for keeping me focused on doing it.

To my son Jonathan and daughter Elizabeth, both of whom were shaped by effective Youth ministry and demonstrate a commitment to people which is pure gift and a model of servant ministry.

Sally's Acknowledgments

Thanks to all who have helped me with this project, particularly Centre for Youth Ministry students, YFC staff and others who answered my emails or completed questionnaires. Special thanks to Malcolm for inviting me to get involved with this booklet and to Paul who always encourages me.

The Cover Illustration is by Peter Ashton

First Impression March 2006
ISSN 0144-171X
ISBN 1 85174 617 X

A Growing Trend

1

Setting the Scene

Good News for Young People, the Church of England National Youth Strategy, suggests that 'It seems to be a justified claim that the Church employs more youth workers than local government.'[1] A Church Life Profile undertaken in 2001 on behalf of a variety of denominations and organizations suggests that around one in six churches has a youth worker, which gives a figure of 6,000 youth workers, about half of whom are full time. The gender split is 56% male and 44% female, contrasting with senior ministers where 85% are male. Age profiles differ too, with two thirds of youth workers being under 40 compared with one in eight senior ministers.[2] Whilst cautioning that a causal link cannot necessarily be proven, the conclusion is drawn that:

> The presence of youth workers is positively associated with a growing sense of belonging within the church, higher numbers of new people attending, more people involved in evangelism, a wide range and greater number of evangelistic outreach activities, higher growth in faith during the last year, greater commitment to the vision of the church, more people involved in youth ministry, higher satisfaction with all young people's and children's activities, a wide range and greater number of welfare and social action activities, a younger age profile for the church, a higher proportion of male attenders and a higher likelihood that the church is growing numerically.[3]

The picture was not uniformly so 'up beat' and three negative associations were identified:

> A less stable sense of belonging within the church, fewer people involved in social welfare outreach activities, fewer newcomers who have returned to church after a long absence.

Unfortunately the reasons for both the positive and negative associations cannot be clearly articulated. However, encouragement is also to be found in Bob Jackson's research. Referring to examples from the Dioceses of Coventry and St Albans, he concludes that:

Although further work on this needs to be done, the figures do suggest that employing professional, specialist staff members is a good practice that at least halts the decline in the numbers of children and young people in the churches. And one would imagine that it also gives them a better quality of Christian learning and experience.[4]

With such a large number of professional specialists engaged in youth ministry, it is helpful to reflect on how the relationship between youth specialist and minister can be enhanced. Part of this involves identifying some of the possible issues and tensions that can arise, as well as looking at areas of good practice that can increase effectiveness and provide the support that is needed. It is encouraging to see a recent online survey suggesting that 'over half of church-based youth workers say the quality of the line management they receive is "good" or "excellent."'[5] However, our own research does not fully back that up. From our different perspectives, Sally as a youth work educator and Malcolm as a clergy educator, we both still hear a regular flow of stories where the experience is not so good. Often when you explore in a little more depth why someone is leaving a post, a contributory factor is relationship difficulties.

Identifying Barriers to Effective Youth Ministry from a Youth Worker Perspective[6]

Some recurring themes emerge when exploring such barriers which may be categorized under four headings, relating to the worker, the clergy, the church and to all three elements. If such obstacles can be identified, then it is usually possible to deal with them. Furthermore, when developing a new post or appointing a new worker, some potential barriers can be thought through in advance and hopefully avoided.

Barriers Relating to the Youth Worker

- Clashes in values, particularly for professionally qualified youth workers
- Feeling that their vision for the work is suppressed
- Difficulty in coping with being constantly in the spotlight
- Feelings of isolation, including few people from their peer group in church
- Blurring of personal and professional boundaries
- Pressures of being a role model
- Coping beyond the honeymoon period and finding the motivation for the long haul

Barriers Relating to the Clergy

- Lack of management and supervision of their youth worker
- Clergy with a more conservative outlook
- Clergy rarely seeing what is done and feeding back secondhand comments
- Decisions being made that affect the youth work and youth worker without them being consulted

Barriers Relating to the Church

- Problems with young people not being allowed to participate fully in the church
- Difficulties with others using the building or trivial complaints by church members
- Lack of ownership of the youth work by the wider church
- Lack of personal spiritual nourishment from the church where they work
- An unwillingness to engage with good practice in issues like child protection
- Church politics, including an unwillingness to tackle issues with particular individuals or families
- Lack of volunteers and over-reliance on paid workers
- Tensions between methodology of informal youth work and usual educational processes in the church

Barriers That Come from All Three Elements

- Unrealistic or unspoken expectations
- Perceptions of status of ordained and lay ministry
- Misunderstandings around the nature of youth work and pressure for 'bums on seats'
- Lack of planning and setting of objectives
- Understandings of what church is
- Differing understandings of vocation and how this is worked out

Not all of these barriers stem from the clergy/youth worker relationship, but it will often be in this context that they need to be worked out. With so many potential obstacles to effective ministry, ways must be found to engage with them and find a productive way to work together. Some barriers may be experienced by both youth workers and clergy, since they are issues for Christian ministry generally. Exploring together some strategies for overcoming them could therefore be of benefit to all parties. Experience suggests that effort in a few crucial areas can help. These especially include good preparation (involving the whole church) before a youth worker is appointed, combined with a commitment to good management, supervision and professional development for the worker.

It is Not Just the Youth Worker that has Issues!

Although this chapter is written mainly from the youth worker's perspective, it is only fair to mention issues raised by churches and clergy too. Steve Tilley assessed four common complaints expressed by clergy he encountered about their youth workers:

- They do not get up early enough in the morning
- They are very untidy and poor at administration
- I never know where they are
- They spend all their time playing on the computer

Some youth workers would certainly own up to some or all of these! In response, Tilley urges churches to ensure that job descriptions, line management, staff meetings and treatment of the worker are all done thoroughly and that the worker's development is a priority.[7]

It would also be naïve to ignore the wider context of the relationship between the youth worker and clergy.[8] The youth worker needs to be aware that clergy have a range of concerns that may impact them and their work. In relation to the church, these include the pressure of all the other demands on their time: parents' expectations of the youth worker; the congregation's perceptions of what the youth worker actually does when much youth work is unseen; church or denominational politics; financial issues and competing priorities; reconciling different visions and understandings of youth work and church. There can also be what they see as problems with the youth worker, for example, tensions when the initial vision and impetus for a project came from within a church, followed by a new youth worker coming in and seeking to make changes to suit his or her own vision; modes of communication and understandings of accountability; working with someone who has a different set of professional skills and values; avoidance of conflict and lack of willingness from the youth worker to deal with interpersonal tensions.

This chapter has sought to highlight some of the concerns and tensions in the clergy/youth worker relationship, mainly from the perspective of the youth worker. The next chapter focuses on the situation from a clergy point of view, especially in the light of how clergy are shaped generally through their training and experience to 'do' church.

Clergy A Part?

2

Snap Shot 1

To gain an informal 'snap shot' of how clergy feel about managing and developing youth ministry, Malcolm carried out an informal survey of 30 clergy in a Church of England diocese in 2002. This diocese has a large number of youth workers, of mixed gender and age, with varied levels of ministry experience and from differing traditions. Despite the fact that the questionnaire was sent out just before Holy Week, within ten days most had been returned.

One respondent (male, middle aged, 'central' Anglican tradition, 17 years' ministry experience) wrote:

> Youth workers need to live on the edge and be seen to be taking risks/chances. They are likely to be dealing with a culture that is substantially different from a classic, English, middle class church (of which I am a part).

Another minister wrote that, even in the context of close working relationships, there would always be tension between those working within and representing the institution and those whose role is to go beyond it, with regard to how the two cultures should relate and interact. It is how this fact is acknowledged and valued, so that the tension ('come to' meets 'go to') can remain a creative one, which has in part given rise to the writing of this booklet.

Another minister wrote that there would always be tension with regard to how the two cultures should relate and interact

After the sense of hope and excitement at the beginning of a church youth worker appointment, both clergy and youth workers can soon feel alienated by the models of leadership and ministry practice offered to them by the other. Amongst the potential barriers to developing effective youth worker/clergy relationships, we saw a number of issues relating to poor leadership, management and communication skills. However, the youth worker will sometimes experience the clergy model of leadership and ministry itself as confining and inappropriate for the practical outworking of their ministry. This is a very real issue, as some clergy have been trained in a particular theological framework for a hierarchical institution. This means it may be increasingly difficult for them to play a formative role in managing and developing youth ministry, struggling to understand its specific nature and its cultural location.[9] What is seen as a 'one dimensional' view of ministry appears no longer adequate, when what is needed is leadership which can help create more flexible patterns of being and doing church.[10] Reasonably self-aware clergy can easily begin to feel incompetent and dispirited in this area of their oversight and ministry, as they struggle to come to terms with a different model of being and doing church.

Our concern is that, even though many youth workers may express a measure of satisfaction with 'their' clergy, there are still a significant number for whom the clergy expectation of 'getting more young people into church' runs counter to their priority in helping young people relate to Jesus. This can mean that problems arise even when management and supervision work well.

There are still a significant number for whom the clergy expectation runs counter to their priority in helping young people relate to Jesus

From the survey responses in Snap Shot 1, it was clear that there was no doubt among clergy that developing youth ministry through the local church is vitally important. However, what did emerge was clergy feeling ill equipped to help shape and manage a ministry which they realize needs to be radically different in shape and practice to their own, if it is to be effective (and even prophetic). The 'big' issue for the church in relation to youth ministry (and beyond), concerns the need to develop an ordained leadership base that not only has relevant leadership skills, but those skills linked with a vision and ability to help shape and manage a participative and relational 'go to' ministry model, through their church communities.[11] This is a major challenge in a context when most clergy have been called, selected, trained and 'shaped' in a 'come to' ministry model, where, more often than not, 'attendance at church services equals faithfulness.'[12] Can a kingdom-based ('go to')[13] ministry work alongside a church-based ('come to') one—especially in a context where church leaders are shaped and driven more by a desire to see more young people 'come to' church? The issue is important, as it is primarily the clergy responsibility to set a context of partnership and collaboration, which will enable the youth worker's ministry to develop professionally and contextually.

'Go to'—the Only Way to Come!

Youth A Part was the first report giving special attention to young people to be considered by the General Synod of the Church of England.[14] In clarifying the extent, nature and purpose of youth work within the Church, it sought to give a theological and missiological framework for youth ministry, within an emerging post-Christendom culture. The report outlined the present situation, demonstrating the Church of England's involvement in the lives of many young people through its historic partnership with educational and voluntary agencies, whilst acknowledging the increasing gap that exists between church and youth cultures beyond these formal agencies.

Although the focus of the report was the role of the church-based youth worker in contemporary Britain, and how this could be understood and resourced more effectively, there are far-reaching implications for those who manage and develop youth ministry in the church, not least the clergy. Recommendations concerning youth involvement in outreach work, young people being trained for leadership, increasing participation by young people in decision-making structures and planning and leading worship, are part of a wider and more fundamental vision. This concerns the creation of a *community and relational context* for young people's increasing participation, which has:

> ...permeable boundaries, where movement towards Christ matters more than the level of commitment achieved; a place where love is indiscriminate.[15]

This report was followed up in 2002 by a National Youth Strategy, which takes the four key elements identified in *Youth A Part* and seeks to develop and implement plans for each area.[16] More recently, the *Mission-shaped Church* report, published in 2004, has reflected much of this understanding, though applying it (rightly) to the wider mission of the church.

To achieve this community and relational context, *Youth A Part* laid down a crucial understanding of church, which speaks not only into youth ministry practice in church and society today, but also has important implications for the clergy/youth worker relationship. In this

Youth A Part sets out an understanding for ministry which, if ignored, goes right to the heart of why clergy and youth ministry may continue to develop 'apart'

very important respect, *Youth A Part* sets out an understanding for ministry which, if ignored, goes right to the heart of why clergy and youth ministry may continue to develop 'apart,' with the church becoming less effective than it already is in penetrating youth (and other) cultures in the UK.

The report describes church culture as being dominated by the 'bounded set' mentality, expressed by the creation of a category with defined characteristics. So, for instance, church is conditioned by certain values, where to belong means to accept certain truths and behave in certain ways. Those who belong are 'one of us,' whilst those who do not are viewed as 'not the same.' For example, most clergy and church members see attendance on a Sunday as *the* sign of membership and commitment. Ministry and mission are thus determined by the ecclesiastical structures and context.

> Following this line, they define 'Christian' in terms of a set of essential, measurable, definitive characteristics—like right doctrine plus right polity plus right action...They have an 'ecclesiastical' approach to evangelism.[17]

However, *Youth A Part* sees the 'centred set' model as the one most appropriate for developing youth ministry in a societal context which has seen a significant change in the overall culture.

> Adolescent popular culture still defines itself against adult culture to a considerable extent; but, in reality, youth culture has been shaped much more significantly by the changes overtaking western culture as a whole.[18]

The 'centred set' consists of those moving *towards* the centre, however distant they may be. The dimension of spiritual growth and commitment to Jesus in discipleship determines nearness to the centre, which is Jesus Christ himself. Because people are viewed in terms of their relationship to the centre, membership is defined more loosely. The concern is not with boundaries, or with who is in and who is out, but with a clear focus on the centre and movement towards it.

Because people are viewed in terms of their relationship to the centre, membership is defined more loosely

Frost and Hirsch make the claim that the mission of the whole church, and not just youth ministry, should be seen as wholly 'Christocentric.'[19] They believe that the two models should not and cannot be mixed. 'If you must stick with the traditional-attractional mode, then you are obligated to see your church as a bounded set.' The main purpose of such a model is to tell people that it is better to be in rather than out. Centred set churches will see ministry and mission being determined more by relationships than by structures. 'Only when a community of faith is prepared to leave its space and enter into another sub-culture will it be able to effectively see itself as, and be, a centred set.'[20]

In terms of youth ministry practice, for many youth workers, including those operating within some larger evangelical churches where the 'come to' model predominates, a 'centred set' model means valuing developing relationships beyond the church door. It means seeing church as emerging from within that, without defining church by corporate attendance located in a building called a church, on a particular day of the week.[21] The key value is movement not uniformity, and boundaries are not defined.

Snap Shot 2

This is based on a real life conversation witnessed by one of the authors. It may be considered extreme by some, but it highlights the sort of issues that can arise when centred set meets bounded set.

The vicar and youth worker from a large evangelical church are discussing a critical issue concerning the strategic development of youth ministry in the parish. An open youth club run by the youth worker and her team, held in the church hall, brings in large numbers of young people from the village and its large comprehensive school, where the youth worker has developed credible links through regular visits. The vicar is concerned that, if this is a church youth club, then there should be some sort of requirement that those who attend should also attend church. For the vicar the significant marks of Christian belonging are a commitment to the church's worship and life, as expressed by (regular) attendance and involvement in church activities. The youth worker, however, appears to be working to an understanding of ministry and church where the key value is relational development and the movement towards Christ within that.[22] The issue of church attendance is not a key one, even if the worship at a particular service is considered to be 'youth oriented.'

3 Mission-shaped Church Means Mission-shaped Clergy

Many issues encountered in the working relationships and respective ministries of clergy and youth workers take on even more importance in the light of current thinking about the missionary nature of the church.

The Church of England has recently sought to respond to its missionary challenge by revising its Criteria for Selection and the exercises it uses to recommend candidates at its selection conferences.[23] In the revision there is a more explicit focus on mission and evangelism, together with leadership and collaboration. The preface notes, 'the current shift of emphasis towards mission (reflected not least in the 2004 report *Mission-shaped Church*) required a new criterion which would assess the skills, attitudes and abilities which relate to the missionary enterprise.'[24]

The criteria now put great emphasis on the concept of the church being part of the 'Missio Dei'

The Mission and Evangelism criterion does require potential ordination candidates to be aware that their vocation or call occurs within a developing post-Christendom context of 'consumerism, choice and convenience' and one in which new approaches to ministry 'need to be explored that are imaginative and flexible.'[25] The criteria now put great emphasis on the concept of the church being part of the *'missio dei'* and that potential candidates will be permeated by the call to mission. They will need to have an awareness of contemporary cultural contexts 'with an ability to reflect on the interaction between culture and gospel.'[26] Alongside this will be a commitment to enable others in mission and evangelism and, generally, for oversight level, evidence of some potential to be a leader in mission.

Consequently, emphasis is now being placed on the ability of potential ministers to work with others in communicating, defining, sharing and working out a corporate vision.[27] This will mean a developing capacity to respond to change and to assist others to embrace it. With regard to the management and development of youth ministry, it is encouraging to note that the criteria recognize that most ministerial contexts now require a 'sophisticated and self-aware' leadership that is able to 'draw on the abilities of others and share responsibility with them.'[28] Further to this, Bishops' Advisers should ascertain that candidates have an 'understanding of leadership, power and interdependence.'[29]

In all this there is a welcome acknowledgment that the world has changed and that the church needs skilled leaders who are looking at the church through 'mission-shaped' eyes. What is now needed is some teasing out of what it means to be a 'leader in mission' and the theological understanding and the skills required to develop a more 'go to' context for all church communities. At the moment it could all feel rather 'bolt-on.'

Some may argue that at this stage this is enough and that the relevant theological understandings and skills can be developed in training and through reflective practice. However, a system as front-loaded as selection for Anglican ordination does require some assurances that the training received will be consistent with developing missional leadership. Some understandably argue that training should be about both/and, but we do need to ensure that a fresh 'centred set' approach at least equates with the prevailing 'bounded set' one.

We do need to ensure that a fresh 'centred set' approach at least equates with the prevailing 'bounded set' one

It is crucial, therefore, that the *Youth A Part* value of 'centred-set ministry' is understood and reflected within the advisory and selection process, as candidates for ordained ministry need to show signs of understanding what a 'centred set/go to' model of church and ministry is about and that, 'a new type of leadership must precede any meaningful transition to missional church.'[30]

In other words, if we want a mission-shaped church we need mission-shaped clergy (including bishops). In a context where the Revised Criteria have been approved and Advisory Panels are up and running, this will require a consistent following through of the revised mission criteria (interpreted in terms of the 'centred set' value as key to what is being looked for in potential 'leaders of mission'[31]) at all levels of the discernment, selection and training process.

In the spirit of thinking outside the Anglican 'box' it might be appropriate to choose Bishop's Advisers from some of the emerging network and generational churches (whether Anglican or not), together with experienced youth ministry practitioners.

The Baptist example of ordaining youth specialists who feel that their long-term vocation is to work among young people is something which may be considered, especially in the light of the 'Pioneer Minister' proposals recently put forward by the Church of England as part of its response to the *Mission-shaped Church* report.

Snap Shot 3

A proposal to develop a network church in a large provincial city, aiming to tap into younger generational cultures and lifestyles, has been accepted by an Anglican diocese. It is seen as church without walls. A business plan was produced to promote the concept and release diocesan funding for a stipend. The aim is to develop a 'centred set/go to' model. For the institutional church, this project is both a challenge and an opportunity: an opportunity to give permission and oversight; and a challenge not to put pressure on leaders for numbers and finance. To do this would simply recreate what we have already got and lead to the mutation of 'attendance equals faithfulness' fairly rapidly. It is this tense dynamic that is, as we have seen, often at the heart of the clergy/youth ministry relationship. At its opening 'service' held in a city centre pub, the author was asked two questions that reflect deeply ingrained 'come to' attitudes. One was 'How many people have come?' and 'How many people from the bar downstairs came up and joined us?' The answer to the latter was to point out that maybe the real question was how many of us went downstairs to join the customers where they were?

The Youth Worker Perspective 4

Perceptions and Frustrations of Ministry

Integral to any ministry are understandings of identity, vocation and lifestyle. Youth workers and clergy may agree on the importance of working out these issues, but can face conflict in reconciling how these concepts are understood and worked out in practice. It should be emphasized that people in ministry have much in common. Edmondson, for example, in his book on sustaining effective ministry, lists Sandford's special difficulties for those in ministry:[32]

- The job is never finished;
- We do not know if our work has any results;
- The work is repetitive;
- We are constantly having to deal with people's expectations;
- We must work with the same people year in and year out;
- Working with people in need saps our energy;
- Many come not for solid spiritual food but for 'strokes';
- We often function behind a mask;
- We can become exhausted by failure.

This list is not definitive and some of the frustrations felt by youth workers over administration, church politics, lack of volunteers, petty complaints, different perceptions of mission and the focus of ministry may all affect clergy too. Staff teams can provide support and encouragement and an atmosphere of honesty and collegiality. They can also form the context where discussions around the ministry undertaken can begin to build a platform to explore some areas of potential tensions in different approaches to identity, vocation and lifestyle. Youth workers need to appreciate that clergy also have ministry issues to contend with, and that they (youth workers) can either add to the problem or be part of a solution.

Real Ministry?

One of the frustrations that some youth workers have is that their vocation as a youth worker is often seen as a stepping stone to 'real ministry.' Some might feel called into other areas of ministry at some point, but many feel that youth ministry is a long-term vocation and feel discouraged at any inference that it is second best or second class. The Centre for Youth Ministry has had students from their late teens to their fifties—youth ministry is not a vocation only for the young. This issue has been addressed by Baptists, who have an ordination route for youth specialists with equivalence of terms and conditions with those who have trained on a general ministerial course.

Shared Conditions of Service

Inequalities in the treatment of clergy and youth workers can be a root of some of the frustrations felt. The premise of some church-based youth workers is that they are functioning in a priestly way with the young people and thus need (and should be offered) the same sorts of opportunities for personal and professional development. The Church of England has guidelines for parishes about caring for the clergy to ensure that they have:[33]

- a safe environment in which to live and work;
- sufficient time off for rest, recreation and proper holidays;
- an annual opportunity to make a retreat of at least a week's duration;
- adequate administrative assistance;
- reimbursement in full of ministerial expenses;
- appropriate release for extra-parochial ministry;
- encouragement for ministry to the whole community and not just to the congregation.

Here you have an excellent starting point for a staff development and support policy that would benefit youth workers as well as clergy

If you add in the diocesan responsibility to provide continuing ministerial education throughout a person's ministry, the recommendation to have support for their spiritual life and a structure for pastoral care, then you have an excellent starting point for a staff development and support policy that would benefit youth workers as well as clergy.

A final point made in the clergy guidelines is that those exercising pastoral care of clergy should 'by word and example actively encourage the clergy to adopt a healthy life-style.'[34] Many youth workers struggle to emulate the life-style adopted by their line managers and are caught between their own understandings of work/life balance and that which they may feel is expected of them. Expectations are often unspoken and may even be unreal, but they can add to the pressures faced by youth workers with an understanding of what it means to be in ministry which differs from their line manager's. Exploring these different perceptions early on in a post can be helpful for all parties.

Thriving Not Surviving

Part of training for ministry is hopefully helping people to identify what they need to thrive, not merely survive. Giving attention to these areas can enhance the youth worker/clergy relationship and enable a more fruitful ministry to take place. Underpinning everything else is respect, trust and freedom to be who they are, an affirmation of their call.

What the Worker Needs

- Effective supervision and feedback that is seen as a priority by the manager.
- Good pastoral support, with appropriate affirmation and encouragement.
- Clear boundaries and expectations known by all stakeholders.
- Time for networking and continuing professional development.
- Time out to reflect and grow.
- A growing relationship with God and space for this to be nurtured in a way that is right for the youth worker, which may be outside of the church they work for.
- To engage in reflective practice, to learn and grow from experiences and setting aside time to do this.

What the Clergy Need To Do

- Impart to youth workers a sense that they are as important as the work and that their well-being, growth and development matters.
- Give the worker the opportunity to develop and implement vision.
- Understand the values and approach of the youth worker and resist 'bums on seats' as the only measure of success.
- Avoid blurring boundaries in the professional parts of the relationship or encouraging youth workers to compromise on what for them are professional principles.

What the Church Needs To Do

- Adequately resource the work, particularly with people and finance.
- Be prepared to make changes for the sake of the youth work rather than always expecting the youth work to make the changes.

Understanding what some of these issues are in a specific situation can help a youth worker to feel valued, understood and affirmed. Underlying all of this is a strong foundation of understanding, management and supervision, which facilitates the discussion and resolution of the issues that have been highlighted thus far. The next chapter focuses on building this foundation.

5 Building a Strong Foundation

20 years of seeking to support youth workers has convinced me that it is not the young people they work amongst that usually lead to workers leaving their post prematurely.

Rather, it is issues relating to management, support and sustainability of a ministerial lifestyle. Good management, supervision and support can make a difference between a worker leaving or staying.

What Can Contribute to Broken Relationships?

There is no guarantee that relationships of mutual respect, encouragement and learning will develop between clergy and youth workers. Differences in age, gender, ethnicity, culture, education, status, personality, values, temperament and tradition can all make clergy/youth worker communication more complex and may be a factor in a poor relationship. This can be exacerbated by other elements, including inadequate communication, lack of self knowledge or self-awareness, personality traits, a poor image of or antagonism towards the other person, differing perceptions of the appropriate scope or intimacy of the relationship, hasty judgments, insensitivity, lack of empathy, mistaken interpretation of the other, or a lack of time, opportunity and effort to build a relationship.

Experience in supporting youth workers suggests that investing time in trying to understand one another better can be very valuable. The Myers Briggs Type Indicator is one tool widely used by Christians and others to help develop better understanding of oneself and one's team colleagues. Just knowing that extraverts sometimes speak without thinking and may not mean what they say (because they need to speak things out to process their thoughts) can be helpful for introverts to know, particularly when they rarely speak without having thought something through first! A willingness to discuss this or Belbin's team roles, for example, can help identify strengths and weaknesses and suggest better ways of working together.[35] Talking about training and sharing understandings of ministry and mission may feel frustrating if other demands are pressing. However, a good relationship, involving mutual respect and attempting to understand one another, can cope better with the pressures of ministry than one that is superficial or tainted by mutual mistrust.

Line Management

Line management has been defined as 'the continuous process by which the manager directs, supports, motivates, protects, checks the work, provides opportunities for systematic review, consults and passes information to and from the worker.'[36] In this, as Ingram and Harris suggest, there needs to be a balance between the needs of the organization, the needs of the worker and the relationship between the worker and manager. If these are out of balance, then problems can arise. Part of the problem can be self-perception or lack of understanding of roles needed in a team context.

Leaders or Managers?

In a church context the word 'leader' is used rather than 'manager.' The word leader often implies that there are followers, but this can be difficult when applied to a staff team context. Adair helpfully notes that 'true leaders do not seek to create followers, but partners.'[37] He suggests that both Jesus and Paul saw those they worked alongside as 'fellow workers' sharing a common goal. This fundamental attitude can make a big difference to the youth worker/clergy relationship within an organization that has often been seen as unhelpfully hierarchical. Living out what it means to be a servant leader encourages others to act in the same way. Part of being a servant leader in a clergy/youth worker context is to offer appropriate management and supervision.

Previous Experience

For many clergy, their first experience of managing staff in a ministry context is with a student on placement or with a curate. One potential danger here is to transfer approaches to supervision in those learning contexts to a youth workers, who may see themselves as peers with their own specialist training in a different discipline from their line manager. Coll highlights three major areas where differences may occur:[38]

- Knowledge, skills and experience;
- Goals, interests and theoretical orientations;
- Religious and personal belief systems.

To explore these issues fully there needs to be a good self-awareness from both parties and a willingness to be honest, open and vulnerable, particularly in the early stages of getting to know each other. Understanding each other and what each brings to the relationship in these sorts of areas can help diminish misunderstandings and conflict.

Misconceptions of the Supervisory Relationship

A common danger in supervisory relationships is that boundaries are blurred, expectations are not clarified and other issues are carried over into the supervisory relationship. As was discussed above, it is essential for the supervisor to see the youth worker as a partner, fellow worker or colleague in the ministry, rather than a subordinate or someone of lesser status. Mutual respect is vital if trust is to be built and the relationship developed in a productive way. Youth workers discuss the difference between being a friend and being friendly. It is helpful if a supervisory relationship is friendly, but possibly dangerous if friendship gets in the way of it functioning properly. This can be on both sides—supervisors not wanting to challenge or supervisees being wary of putting additional pressure on the supervisor through asking for help, for example. Pastoral support and spiritual direction for the supervisee is also best facilitated outside of the supervisory relationship. This can bring some tensions for clergy whose primary motivation is pastoral and who see their youth worker as someone they have spiritual responsibility for. However, experience from youth workers suggest that the boundaries can get blurred and what they thought was a pastoral confidence shared is then used in another context.

It is essential for the supervisor to see the youth worker as a partner in the ministry, rather than a subordinate

What is Supervision?

Supervision provides a structured opportunity for people to discuss their work. As Thompson says:

> Effective supervision can often be the difference between success and failure; stress and job satisfaction; worry and reassurance; good practice and excellent practice. Its significant role should therefore not be underestimated.[39]

In reviewing some of the literature on supervision it is clear that there are four key areas involved in supervision:[40]

- Management, including accountability, sometimes referred to as 'normative';
- Education and professional development—sometimes referred to as 'formative';
- Support—sometimes referred to as 'restorative';
- Mediation when necessary.

Management involves oversight of the work and has a quality control function, including such things as standard setting, adherence to 'agency' policy and procedures and picking up on mistakes. Education and staff development includes facilitating and promoting learning, helping to identify training needs, developing skills and understanding and abilities. Support includes reflecting on how the work is affecting the individual, dealing with emotions, creating a safe place to discuss issues, sharing burdens, debriefing and ensuring the worker has what they need. Mediation may at times be necessary and, in this context, may be between the worker and the congregation or the worker and other leadership structures. Good supervision will involve all of these elements, but there is a danger that supervisors focus more on the area that is their interest at the expense of others.

There is a danger that supervisors focus more on the area that is their interest at the expense of others

Starting Right

Things may go wrong in a job from day one, but a carefully designed, appropriate, induction programme can help to prevent this. This important component in good employment practice gives an opportunity for a clear statement of principles and practical guidelines to be articulated and understood from the outset. It can be easy to forget what is needed to allow one to function effectively in an organization after one has been there a while.[41] There is further material on the Grove web site about supervision contracts, content of supervision sessions and the responsibilities of supervisors and supervisees.

Potential Relationship Problems

We all bring baggage from our past into relationships and the line manager/ worker relationship is no different. A range of psychological 'games' that can get played out in this context has been identified and it is worth exploring them here briefly, in the hope that in recognizing them they can be avoided or finished.

Morrison talks about the 'conflict between what is going on over the table and what is going on under the table.'[42] He sees the Drama Triangle, which originated from Transactional Analysis, as one of the most common games. The triangle shows three psychological positions that can be adopted, usually as a defence mechanism, to avoid conflict or personal responsibility. Those involved in the triangle adopt a position according to what is happening at the time. Youth workers often seem to feel that they are the victim, being persecuted by the clergy who may switch into pastoral mode and turn into a rescuer.

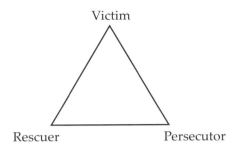

Victim

Rescuer   Persecutor

Being aware of such 'games' can help avoid getting into them. Other possible 'games' include:[43]

Clergy to Youth Worker

'They won't let me' — I would like to agree to what you are asking but the church are not ready for that yet.

'Poor me' — I am sorry about having to cancel supervision but I am so busy with this major pastoral crisis.

'Remember who is boss' — artificially asserting power or seeking to manipulate.

'I'm only trying to help' — seeking to deflect criticism.

'Father or mother knows best' — acting in a patronizing or parental manner.

Youth Worker to Clergy

'I did like you told me' and look what happened — avoiding responsibility.

'If you only understood youth work principles like I do' — reducing power disparity and asserting specialist knowledge.

'I know it's my session but you do look terrible' — trying to reverse roles.

Can apply to Either

'Let's sort it out over a pint' — redefining the relationship or seeking to move from a professional approach.

This chapter has sought to highlight some of the practical ways in which clergy and youth worker relationships can be established, developed, improved and maintained, as well as some of the dangers to look out for.

Getting it Together 6

We hope that this booklet has helped to identify and deal with some of the glitches that arise when people from different backgrounds and 'ecclesiological' understandings come together to establish and work to a common vision.

We have explored the relationship between the youth worker and ordained minister from two related perspectives. One is the outworking of the professional relationship between youth worker and minister, with the need for a measure of skill in terms of management, supervision, communication and expectations. The other perspective concerns the need for the working relationship to be rooted in a shared understanding of the nature of the ministry and mission of the church.

The contention of *Youth A Part,* and, to a lesser extent, of *Mission-shaped Church,* is that, if youth ministry is to be more than just bringing young people into church or keeping existing young people 'on board,' then there needs to be a wholehearted understanding and embracing of 'centred set/go to' perspectives of being and doing church. Our contention here is that, since many clergy are selected and trained within a fairly traditional 'bounded set/come to' church context, it would seem difficult for things to change enough to respond to the missionary challenges facing the church in a 'post-Christendom' consumer-driven world. Youth workers are in many ways the ones 'on the edge,' the 'prophetic' voices we need to listen to and understand. This is key to their ministry development and to the mission of God amongst younger generations.

How then, with increasing numbers of churches employing youth workers, can the potential for effective youth ministry be maximized? We have identified some potentially helpful areas in this. Some are the youth worker's responsibility, others the clergy's and some are appropriate for both to commit to.

Youth workers need to seek to understand the wider context they are working in, including the issues and pressures the clergy face. Participation in management and supervision structures should be helpful, open and constructive and begin with the attitude of thinking the best of others. Wider support is important and the youth worker should ensure that they have identified someone to meet with who offers non-managerial supervision or support.

Some find that one person is helpful in both professional and spiritual areas. Others prefer two people, a spiritual director (or equivalent) and someone with a youth work background to provide non-managerial supervision.

Clergy need to ensure that there is a proper job description and that expectations have been clearly spelt out. An effective support and accountability structure should be put in place, including a line manager who may not always be the main church leader—in a collaborative ministry context there may be someone else who would be more effective. Supervision needs adequate time and a high commitment. It also requires willingness to encourage as well as to challenge and to be there as a sounding board. It is also helpful to provide a holistic view and help the youth worker see a different perspective. Trusting your youth worker is important, being willing to let them take risks, yet supporting them if they fail. Seeing the youth worker as a partner in the ministry, with a complementary set of skills is helpful and far more empowering for them.

Both clergy and youth workers need to have an attitude of wanting to learn from each other. In the initial stages, spending some social or informal time together to get to know each other can be useful. Setting out the vision, values and expectations that each has is beneficial and helps mutual understanding. Spending time theologically reflecting together, and coming to shared, owned decisions where appropriate, helps build a common approach to ministry. Many of us do not like conflict, but we should not collude in avoiding conflict or issues that need resolving. Both parties should have a commitment to say what they mean to each other, rather than talking behind each other's backs. Conflict can also be creative and be the means to moving to a more effective place in ministry —just as 'storming' comes before 'performing' in group work theory. Patience is vital, as it takes time for relationships of trust to grow and it is important to try to avoid prematurely giving up because things do not seem to be working out as was hoped. It can be worthwhile to try to identify frustrating limitations or weaknesses in each other, and seek solutions together, or at least come to a place of acceptance and understanding. A commitment from both parties to communicate and to follow through on decisions and actions helps establish a mutual relationship that can be the basis of a fruitful working partnership.

Some Recommendations

For Training

- Training for clergy and other line managers in recruitment, management and supervision.
- Training for clergy and other line managers in leadership for 'centred set'/'go to' models of being and doing church.

- Consider what can be learnt for clergy training from the models and curriculum for training youth ministers, whether initially or as part of continuing ministerial education.

For Structure and Support

- Diocesan Youth Officers or equivalent should be available to support both the worker and the manager and to help churches in setting up a new post.
- Have appropriate policies in place, including employment-related ones, such as staff development, grievance and disciplinary procedures, as well as work-focused ones like child protection and health and safety.

In Ministerial Practice

- Use tools such as Myers Briggs and Belbin to help to get to know each other and to function effectively as a team.
- Spend time together sharing vision, dreams, passion for ministry and try team away days to explore this in depth.
- Theologically reflect together as a way of trying to find answers to dilemmas that either or both of you face.
- Work towards parity in terms and conditions of service for all in the ministry team.

Multidisciplinary working is the trend in many people-centred professions. It is also perhaps a trend the church should gladly adopt, because the creativity and kingdom potential of colleagues from different disciplines working together is immense. There is an increasing number of professionally qualified youth workers who feel a long-term commitment to church ministry and see themselves as fully qualified for this role, without being ordained but still seeing themselves as equal partners in mission and ministry.

Such youth workers would flourish, working alongside those who, having shown potential at selection and having been further shaped in training by mission-centred theological models and leadership skills, are able to work together with a youth team to affect, influence and sometimes even change the direction of community living. Clergy, who have the power to envision and help create, with others, missionary communities and networks that do not call young people, 'to where they were, and do not try to call them to where…we as church are…as beautiful as that place might seem to us…but…have the courage to go with them to a place that neither you nor they have ever been before.'[44] A Church that enables young people to be rooted in Christ and to be able to live for him 'in the everyday world of their peers.'[45]

Bibliography

John Adair, *The Leadership of Jesus* (Norwich: Canterbury Press, 2001)

Archbishops' Council, *Criteria for Selection in the Church of England* (London: Church House Publishing, 2005)

Archbishops' Council, *Mission-shaped Church* (London: Church House Publishing, 2004)

Meredith Belbin, *Team Roles at Work* (Oxford: Butterworth-Heinemann, 1993)

Board of Education and Board of Mission, *Good News for Young People: The Church of England's National Youth Strategy* (London: Archbishops' Council, 2001)

David Brown, *Youth Ministry Stress, its Causes, Effects and Management within the Diocese of Canterbury* (Project for YMCA College Diploma in Management, 2001)

Church of England, *Guidelines for the Professional Conduct of the Clergy* (London: Church House Publishing on behalf of the Convocations of Canterbury and York, 2003)

Chris Cocksworth and Rosalind Brown, *Being a Priest Today* (Norwich: Canterbury Press, 2002)

Regina Coll, *Supervision of Ministry Students* (Collegeville: Liturgical Press, 1992)

Graham Cray, *Postmodern Culture and Youth Discipleship* (Grove Pastoral booklet, P 76)

Steven Croft, *Ministry in Three Dimensions* (London: Darton, Longman and Todd, 1999)

Vincent Donovan, *Christianity Rediscovered* (London: SCM-Canterbury Press, 1982)

Chris Edmondson, *Fit to Lead: Sustaining Effective Ministry in a Changing World* (London: Darton, Longman and Todd, 2002)

Michael Frost and Alan Hirsch, *The Shaping of Things to Come* (Peabody:

Hendrickson Publishers, 2003)

Alison Gelder and Philip Escott, *Profile of Youth Workers*, Churches To-gether in England Co-ordinating Group for Youth Work (London: Private Report, 2003)

Eddie Gibbs and Ian Coffey, *Church Next* (Leicester: IVP, 2001)

David Green and Maxine Green, *Taking A Part—Young People's Par-ticipation in the Church* (London: National Society/Church House Publishing, 2000)

Matt Hall, *Scottish Youth Workers on the Edge: A Participative/action Re-search Report* (Glasgow: FYT, 2002)

Peter Hawkins and Robin Shohet, *Supervision in the Helping Professions* (Buckingham: Open University Press, 2nd ed, 2000).

Bob Jackson, *Hope for the Church* (London: Church House Publishing, 2002)

Gina Ingram and Jean Harris, *Delivering Good Youth Work* (Lyme Regis: Russell House, 2001)

Tony Morrison, *Staff Supervision in Social Care* (Brighton: Pavilion, 1993)

Steve Tilley, *Full-time youth workers: How do we manage one?* (CPAS , 1999 http://www.evangelism.uk.net/papers/youth_worker_3.htm accessed 10/06/2004).

Neil Thompson, *People Skills* (Basingstoke: Macmillan, 1996)

Pete Ward, *Liquid Church* (Carlisle: Paternoster, 2002)

Notes

1   Board of Education and Board of Mission, 2002, p 1.
2   Gelder and Escott, 2003, pp 4–5.
3   Gelder and Escott, 2003, p 21.
4   Jackson, 2002, p 102.
5   John Buckeridge, *Youthwork,* November 2005, p 13.
6   Sources for this chapter are Sally's 20 years in YFC training and supporting youth workers, CYM contacts including Diocesan Youth Officers and equivalents, a project in the Diocese of Canterbury and research undertaken by Frontier Youth Trust in Scotland.

7   Work done on behalf of the Church Pastoral Aid Society, an Anglican organization.

8   This material was gathered from Diocesan Youth Officers and others who have a wider responsibility for youth workers.

9   Guildford Clergy Informal Survey.

10 Croft, 1999, p 41.

11 *Mission-shaped Church*, 2004, p 12.

12 Pete Ward, 2002, p 17.

13 *Mission-shaped Church*, 2004, p 12.

14 *Youth A Part*, 1996.

15 *Youth A Part*, 1996, p 38.

16 Board of Education and Board of Mission, 2002.

17 Monica Hill in *Entering the Kingdom*, as quoted in *Youth A Part*, 1996, p 14.

18 *Youth A Part*, 1996, p 27.

19 Frost and Hirsch, 2003, p 226.

20 Frost and Hirsch, 2003, p 50.

21 *Youth A Part*, 1996, p 15.

22 *Youth A Part*, 1996, p 14f.

23 *Criteria for Selection,* The Archbishops' Council, 2005.

24 Bishop John Went, The Archbishops' Council, 2005 p v.

25 The Archbishops' Council, 2005, p 36.

26 The Archbishops' Council, 2005, p 37.

27 The Archbishops' Council, 2005, p 26.

28 The Archbishops' Council, 2005, p 28.

29 The Archbishops' Council, 2005 p 28.

30 Frost and Hirsch, 2003, p 166.

31 The Archbishops' Council, 2005 p 28.

32 *Fit to Lead*, 2002, p 26.

33 *Guidelines for the Professional Conduct of the Clergy*, 2003, pp 10–11.

34 *Guidelines for the Professional Conduct of the Clergy*, 2003, p 12.

35 Many dioceses, retreat houses and other agencies run introductory Myers Briggs courses. For further information on Belbin see Meredith Belbin, *Team Roles at Work* (Oxford: Butterworth-Heinemann, 1993).

36 Ingram and Harris, 2001, pp 105–7.

37 *The Leadership of Jesus,* 2001, p 117.

38 *Supervision of Ministry Students,* 1992, p 22.

39 *People Skills,* 1996, p 49.

40 Neil Thompson's *People Skills* is an accessible introduction to a range of effective practice in the caring professions. Peter Hawkins and Robin Shohet provide a more complex discussion of supervision.

41 The Grove web site includes details of a possible induction programme.

42 *Staff Supervision in Social Care,* 1993, p 92.

43 See Morrison, ch 5 and Hawkins and Shohet, ch 4 for further details.

44 Donovan, 1982, p xix.

45 Cray, 1998, p 21.